Echoes of the Mind

By

Chuma Mmeka

All Poems by Chuma Mmeka

Copyright © 2015 by Chuma Mmeka

Preface

Echoes of the Mind is a collection of standard poems written by Chuma Mmeka. The work dwells on poetic themes that range from personality, and the patriotic, to friendship, satire, marriage, child protection, sadness and death.

Well written with insightful narratives, the book inspires a broad readership and is indeed a modern reference material to serve collectors and lovers of free minded style poetry.

To my parents and siblings

No love lost, none gained

"I voiced my thoughts

But they failed to listen;

Let me now pen it to paper

And hope they'll someday read".

- Chuma Mmeka *(June 21, 2002)*

We Are Not Equal

"We're both equal" My girl once told me

But she stayed home with modern toys

When I toil out, sweating in the money.

I know another who says we are equal,

Yet she grew up with her both parents

While mine broke up before I toddled.

"We are all equals!" A man again screamed

But the other was born in a private ward

And he, in a dingy health center.

"Man was made equal" a book does preach

Mocking equality and justice for one who is master

And the other born to be his slave.

Who says we are equal?

When the younger may be blessed over the elder,

To become both Heir and Prince.

Speak not again of equals

For some may make money and die in their prime

While others stretch out their wretchery till old age.

Of course, we can't all be equals

When mercy may be shown to whom He wills,

And another perishes for a misdemeanor.

Man will never be equal,

For some are chosen as sheep to be led

Under the perceived wisdom of traitors or gods.

Not Because I'm Gemini

I was born on the twenty first of June

And some wrote my birth date as boon

"He's born on the cusp of the moon";

A gazer actually saw me to be a "goon"

After a led pastor said I'd be "tycoon".

They say I'm Gemini - I beg to disagree,

Such cannot not make a man strong.

It is his acquired life skills and prong,

The inherent talents, they make him be

It's not because they say he's Gemini".

Yes, I love to read, and I love to write

I know a few hear my poetry speak.

Protecting children gives me the kick

I blend my artist side with the activist

I worked for it; it's not a Gemini's gist.

I'm real, I'm always willing to explore;

I can bake, I organize events and I act,

I sing, I'm fit, I also play chess with tact;

Reality and my exposure made me more

Not an idealistic zodiac or worship bore.

Don't bother with raising sentiments:

I'm tired of religion as well as astrology,

Both are pawns in this life's dirty orgy.

I believe in myself and I do my stints,

But I never dwell on unrealistic glints.

Stop The Hard Knocks

Hard knocks do not

Make better people.

Hard Knocks only push up

Dissent and heady attitude

Yes! You may knock them

When they are wrong

But then, not too hard

That they'll never forget.

Once Like A Pearl

My Dear Kerl,

You were once like a pearl:

Holed in oysters from the whirl

And swept up from oceans' swirl.

You were once a gem and a girl,

The graceful belle for an Earl;

But common men did you twirl,

Turning you into sport and spoil.

The Safe Child

The safe child project for a better tomorrow

Campaign against the abuse of the child

A little prayer can change all our lives

Help to better the lives of all children

We need your love, we need your support

Help us now, help us please.

The Free Minds

"All hole na hole!" it was Joe who argued strongly

"That's not true" his friend Dan weakly countered

With no compromise in sight, they argued on and on

Drinking cold brands of beer served with goat meat.

Still on his point, Joe asks "What really matters here?

Is it not just for getting the release and satisfaction?

That I know I can get from every hole that takes me;

And to me, they are always basically the same thing".

Not ready to back out, Dan mocked him some more

"Release and satisfaction for who? *You abi*?

That's selfishness man; I'm disappointed in you Joe"

Downcast, Dan hissed aloud and turned to his drink.

"You don't behave like you know me well" Joe retorts

"You have heard gals moan and scream in my strafing

And in case you don't know brother, let me teach you

A woman's wetness is her release and I get plenty of it".

He pauses for a moment and proudly beams with a smile

He puffed up as if meaning to say "I've won the argument"
And as everyone now to stare at him, he willingly boasted
"I'm the man, you see, anytime; the real one for the ladies".

While the beer dredged friends argued back and forth
Their group of drinking mates sat and quietly watched,
They all listened keenly but then, with growing irritation
And some began to chit chat with others by their side.

Suddenly, Iyke - the always formal one they called 'Tiish'
Spoke up as if in aid of Dan; he pointed at Joe and asked
"How many pussies do you think you have really seen?"
The intrusion into the argument took everyone by surprise.

Quite irked, Joe looked at Tiish and answered annoyingly
"Wetin wan cause this one? Eh guy, you no know me again?
Which kain hole I never see for this country? Fair o, black o;
Tall gal, fat gal, slim, short; how many? Make I begin count?"

The table laughed at the outburst before Dan interjected
"Why then is it that you can't keep any of them for long?
Why are your girls always ready to jump out of your ship
Even if it means drowning in your own friends' beds?"

That one hit Joe below the belt and he glares at Dan

There was more laughter, but Tiish wasn't done yet,

He went on to say "That's not what I meant Big Joe",

Then pausing, he called the attention of the barman.

Tiish made a sweeping gesture to the barman

Who hurried off to replace the table's drinks

Just then, Tiish emptied his glass and continued

"I meant: How many holes have you looked at?"

Shaking his head in disbelief, Joe sat up straight

He looks intensely at Tiish and says "*Na wa for you o!*

Why would a Prince bend to look into a woman's pussy?

I'm meant to pump fire into them, not look at their holes".

But for Cynthia and Angel: the only girls at the table

And then, Dan and Iyke who were both warming up

The rest of the mates including Chibuzor, Maruwa,

Ayo, Gogo, Dave and Louis seemed agreed with Joe.

They nodded vigorously in concord with his analogy;

Just as the barman brought in the requested drinks

And moved round to serve the table of jolly drinkers,
Craig David's 'I met this gal on Monday' blared out.

As the tune came on, Joe jumped up from his seat
He looked at the DJ and shouted "*Give am belle*"
The music volume increased and Joe danced on
The rest watched delightfully as he did his thing.

 Everyone swayed to music as the track played
They all seemed to welcome Joe's comic relief
Two noisy tracks also ran like a long, long time
Before the volume cut down and calm returned.

Joe then threw a head towards the conveniences
Still staggering in his euphoria, he made to go on
But giggling Cynthia pulled him back and said
"Do you have complete papers for your new car?"

To this Joe laughed and replied "Yes of course my baby"
Still holding on firmly to his arm, she asked him again
"Without all your particulars and the right accessories
Would a new car still be termed as being road worthy?"

"I don't think so my dear....of course not" he answered
With this reply, Cynthia let go of his arm and then said
"*Okay na, make you go free your piss first come back,*
I get better lecture for your own important hearing".

As Joe left, the beer drinking mates went quiet awhile
It was Tiish who first caught up on Cynthia's questions
He burst into belly aching laughter and commended her
"*That one good Cynthia, really*; I can't wait to hear you".

Dan seemed to realize it also for he was quick to add
"Yeah, I agree too; that's the very kind of line he wants"
The rest of the mates looked up at the three puzzled
Scouring their bright faces and conspiratory smiles.

Cynthia looked at Angel, winked and simply advised
"*Girl, take am easy please with this your Big Stout oo.*
No mind these our guys and their replacement bottles
If not, you fit no go come waka house again today o".

A tipsy Angel looked uneasy as she responded
"*My sister, na the very third bottle be this one o.*
After this one, I no go do another again, abeg.

I get interview tomorrow, I no want hangover".

It was Gogo who was seated right beside Angel
He closed in and slung an arm over her shoulder
In a richly sexy baritone he then said "Don't worry,
"Enjoy yourself; I will personally drop you at home".

He wanted to continue but was unable to finish
For he was quickly interrupted by his buddy Ayo
Who crackled his knuckles noisily and said simply
"Think of driving yourself home first my man".

With everyone's attention now centered on him,
Ayo drank from his glass first before he reported
"See this dude o, he actually passed out yesterday
He couldn't even drive himself home from the club".

Ayo wasn't finished yet as he still continued
"It took Louis and me to get him into my car
I drove him to my house where he spent the night;
It was this morning he went to pick up his jalopy".

Gogo threw a playful punch at Ayo who ducked

Every other person at the table laughed out aloud

Just about then, Joe returned to them and asked

"Wetin cause the laugh? The alcohol dey work abi?"

As Joe took his seat, he shouted at the barman

"Ijomah, replace our drinks I beg you" he said

Sharp sharp, no dulling; no time for dull moments"

At the command, the barman scurried to the task.

Angel shook her head twice before she huskily said

"Not for me, I have an important interview tomorrow"

"O come on, one more won't kill you" Joe persuaded

"I don't know o..." Angel said and glanced at Cynthia.

Cynthia took up the challenge, directing a jab at Joe

"She say she no go drink again eh, you go force am?"

"No." Joe replied, "I am more interested in car papers

And why you've joined forces to interrogate me today?

Cynthia began to reply, but Joe bade her wait for him

"You go now come explain whether you be Angel mama"

As if to create suspense, Cynthia stared first at Joe

Then she cleared her throat and swigged from her glass.

She swallowed the gulp, looked square at Joe and said
"Guy fashi this your interrogation and mama talk abeg
Na true life lecture na im I wan give you; nothing do you"
She emptied her glass and refilled it, ready to continue.

She searched his face; sure of his attention, she began
"All hole no be hole my brother, na true talk I dey tell you;
Some holes get particulars wen others no come get"
Cynthia paused and Joe asked "What do you mean?"

They were both in control of the talk, but she responded
"Don't you worry; I will come to my meaning in a moment"
Cynthia glanced at each person on the table and tasked
"Who knows the full meaning of the acronym FGM?"

The mates but three shook heads oblivious of the acronym
"Is it Federal Government related?" Marwa did attempt
"No" Tiish proffered, "It means Female Genital Mutilation"
"I know you know Tiish" Cynthia said "but this is my lecture".

Continuing, Cynthia launched into a clearly informed speech
"Yes, female genital mutilation remains a very huge problem
It's the greatest scourge of all time against the girl child, and

A great percentage of women in Africa's been ruined by it".

"Genital mutilation is the apex of man's inhumanity to woman;
It's attributed to obnoxious tradition and promiscuity excuse".
The mates all waited in anticipation to hear Cynthia speak out
While she paused, drank from her glass, still poised to continue.

"I'm a victim and till tomorrow, I hate myself and parents for it;
I still wonder if I'll ever forgive them for letting it happen to me
And for the many pains the invasion has caused me in this life"
The mates were now transfixed, but she continued undaunted.

"Yes o! This my own *hole no get better relevant particulars*
Sex for me can thus be a bore, an actual pain in the arse"
She paused as if to let that sink in before turning back to Joe
"I get wet, even pleasure; but only a horse can take me there".

Some of the mates blinked rapidly, shifty on their bar seats
The one they called Tiish giggled boyishly but was interested
Angel seemed more amenable to taking yet another drink,
And Joe fixed his gaze and finger to something on his glass.

One did not find such open minded opportunities everyday

And in Africa, sexual opinions by women always seem odd

It was indeed delightful to hear a woman freely speak out

So they all availed Cynthia the audience to spend her speech

She did not disappoint them as she continued shortly

"It'll take a horse to bring me the orgasm I only dream about;

Some of those girls who scream and shout for you sometimes

Cry out of pain from your machismo or a baseless masochism".

A night light shined reflectively, revealing the mist in her eyes

Yet unabashed and bold, Cynthia was still clearly not done

As she again downed her drink, she made to take her bottle

But oddly quiet Dave beat her to it as she murmured "Thanks".

Cynthia continued while still watching the carefully done refill

"It takes much much more than just thrusting in and out of me,

 No matter how long or hard, to take me up to the ninth cloud;

Most men will only end up bruising me, my flesh and emotion".

Joe the smooth talker was now clearly getting discomforted

He heaved then and exclaimed "Meeen" to everyone's hearing

Angela had declined the drink brought by the fine boy barman

She now signaled to the eavesdropping guy to get her a stout.

Cynthia hadn't really stopped; she just stepped up the gist

"All because a most sensitive part of my physical particulars

Was chopped off after I was born as complete as God made me;

They'd hoped to check promiscuity and make a good wife of me".

"Perhaps they were right, for I can do without the thrusting sex

Yet in allowing that choice, my parents did me a great injustice

For I now do not look forward to becoming anybody's wife.

With the demands of wifehood by some, I will rather be damned".

A hiccup caught up with her rapid and emotion laden lecture

She stopped and called for water which was brought promptly

She drank from the bottle, exhaled a breath and then declared

"My elder sister died in childbirth as a result of circumcision".

"My mother now behaves as if she does regret all of that

But then, my well educated father should have known better

My mother went through excruciating pains in child delivery

Losing blood and a baby because she too was circumcised".

"They were the ones who told and ceaselessly reminded us,

Yet they both subjected us to painful lifelong punishment"

Cynthia went quite awhile and a cold draft pervaded the air
The barman brought Angel's drink, but Cynthia didn't mind.

Tiish drank from his mug to wet his throat and said with glee
"You see Joe, take time to inspect those hundreds of holes,
You may find they don't look the same; some look pretty wild
Others remain plain simple. Check it out, you will understand".

Everyone smiled and Cynthia hushed Tiish with a wave of hand
She tapped Angel on the shoulder and said "Time to go home gal"
And to Dave she looked and said "*Guy, you go drop us oo, abeg*"
Then she fully looked Big Joe in the face in obvious cut finality.

"Joe before I go, I am not saying I never achieve sexual pleasure
But truth is, with my manmade condition and your orientation
A traditional Prince like you cannot just afford to give it to me
For it takes skills, not just macho to get me high and kicking".

At this, some of the mates heaved and some noisily shuffled
While some stood up in unison, others kept sitting to pay bills
They all reflected on what had been said, and got ready to go
But as they left the bar as one, other antics began to play out.

Throes of Orphans

My name is Chi

His name is Chu

He is an orphan,

I am an orphaness.

I am eight years old,

My brother is just five.

Our parents are dead,

We don't why they should die.

Papi was sick for a long time,

Mami too, but she was stronger.

Papi died first,

Mami said it was poison -

Our uncle was responsible.

Then Mami followed,

Giving birth to baby.

They say baby was a witch

Who killed her mother.

That day when baby came,

Mami was lying on the floor

She was screaming for help

But no one seemed to hear.

I rushed to call auntie,

But everywhere was dry -

She was at the market already.

I raced back to Mami,

She looked at me,

But she did not talk.

I called her, she did not answer.

She just looked and looked,

I moved, yet she looked ahead.

Chu was lying beside her,

He held mami's hand and cried.

Under mami, there was blood,

So much than I had ever seen.

I raised mami's skirt to see,

Baby was there moving small small.

I was too afraid to touch,

I could not even speak.

When I did not move,

I saw that the baby too had stopped.

I now poked it and poked again,

But she didn't move at all.

I didn't know what to do,

So I broke down and cried.

It was after sunset,

When auntie came to see us.

The door was wide open,

So she just walked in.

I was still there crying,

But no tears on my face.

Chu was now sleeping,

Still holding on to mami.

Auntie's scream showed me,

That all I'd seen was real.

She ran out and came back,

With three other people.

They took mami and baby,

To where I do not know.

They refused to tell me,

Or listen to Chu's cries.

We slept without food,

Still in the mess of blood.

When morning came,

Was when they struck.

Wicked men and women,

Burnt our thatched house.

They let us watch,

While they razed down our hut.

Then they told us to go -

Very far and never come back.

They called our parents evil,

A curse to their land.

They all watched -

Uncle and auntie with them,

As we walked away

Soaked in our own tears.

We walked and walked,

Not knowing where to go.

We finally stopped at another village,

To sleep and beg for food.

We moved into the bush,

And I built a plantain cover -

Where Chu and I,

Finally laid to rest.

We lived there for long,

Eating fruits and cracking nuts.

We would go for days without bath,

Until we could sneak to the stream.

It was so until a kind auntie

Came close and chose to help us.

She brought us food and water,

And got some men to fix a hut.

To help us she said,

We will always come to her house.

We did that on everyday's morning -

When she would give us chips and water,

To go and sale at the motor park.

When we came back everyday,

She would give us some food and drink,

At a time, she did give us some clothes.

We always return her proceeds,

We never lost any.

But when she said Chu must go to city,

We refused and she was angry.

She refused to again help us,

Or let us sell for her.

I begged her and we cried,

But she refused to hear.

So once again, we were on our own.

I took water from another woman

And we began to sell again.

With the money we made,

We bought food and stuff.

This is how we lived until the police came,

They said the government sent them,

To put us in school.

They took me, they took Chu

And all the other children within.

They brought us here and said,

We must bring our parents.

My Gem

You're just like a pearl,

Taken from an oyster's soil;

I'll keep rubbing you to shine,

And know you're truly mine.

I'll walk tall with you as dame,

My own most lustrous gem;

The Icon of beauty and grace,

I found in the deeper most place.

Keep My Heart

I love you, let me now be terse

My heart is no longer my own;

I've given it to you, it's no farce

Hold it well, do not put it down.

Trust me, when I say I'm yours

It's a promise I sure won't fail;

I believe in you, it wasn't by force

It's a clear story anyone can tell.

I had prayed for quite so long

Waiting for that someone right;

Now that you do to me belong

I know the future remains bright.

Higher Glory

I want to be your close friend,

But it's only if you'll come to me;

Do not fear, I will not be a fiend

I'll be a buddy, your own very gee.

I know your innermost pains,

I feel them all just like you do;

But I'll only better your gains,

If you will promise not to boo.

Just walk in through that gate

Let's be sure you're not forced;

I'll change your course of fate

And what I give shan't be paused.

Embrace this one time chance,

Let me give you a new life story;

Come, join in my sacred dance

Let me take you to higher glory.

Hello Dear Friend

Hello Dear Friend,

I know you still glow;

I really want you to know

You're my dear friend indeed.

You bring smiles to my face

Anytime my emotions go bad;

You magnify my happiness

If only to make me feel glad.

Thanks! You are great as can be -

Putting up with my virtues and vice;

Caring, forgiving even when you see

Through all my many pranks and guise.

Keep Glowing My Dear Friend.

For the shine in you multiplies;

Lighting up in others, a light trend

Deserving of a one-world prize.

A Poem For Betty

Dearest Betty,

I really must thank you -
You make much meaning to life;
For though I pay the world my due,
You are the one to keep me from grief.

My memory says thank you:
From the clocking of a Tchar's student,
To the ally sticking in timeless glue -
Our own bond of fun, regrets and a flint.

I have much to thank you for:
The faith in me from a lasting past;
A friendship rooted in hardcore,
With trust - so cemented, so iron cast.

Why won't I show gratitude?
When mindful instances come to me:
Like the ordeal with a stabber dude,
And the push up to keep me be.

You are well appreciated,

For being a dear friend true:

Firm even when wronged,

Never willing to cause a rue.

Indeed, you are my humanity's pride -

With the downs and breaks you've known;

The exuding love none can deride,

And then Alex: who was not let down.

I am happy you now glow:

Waltzing over dim yesteryears,

Picking yourself from sorrow,

Turning the past into brighter days.

Accept my thanks dear Betty,

Know I will always be there;

And though humans can be petty -

With me, you'll have nothing to fear.

Rich And Poor Justice

Why must we get poorer

When they just grow richer?

Why must we strive and sweat

Only for them to claim the fete?

Why should we daily go out first

Yet not rise up beyond their waist?

We get to the bank to queue first

They're late, yet leave fast with zest.

In school, we are only the best

When we work hard without a rest;

They won't work, but they pass

Paying their way, they turn me to crass.

In the hospital, we wait to make a deposit

They get surgery with the speed of rocket.

We buy in the open market feeling reaped

They come, they buy and the seller is tipped.

When it rains, they shelter in fine cars

But we have to cluster in a leaking bus.

They fly across the nation in an hour

We go by road and travel further.

When we die, we are given two weeks

They die, and take months to gather monks.

At the funeral, theirs is a party

But our burial is so ratty.

But at last, judgement comes -

In the grave, there's no boss

And in a six feet bed we all shall lie

Sweet justice that money cannot buy.

No Perfect Marriage

There's no such thing as a perfect marriage

What you package is what you will get

Learn to love and keep her, she's your image

And let her honor him as head of state

Remember you come from different mothers

And that your genes are not the same

Forget the way it was done by your fathers

And try hard to build up your own name

Never make her think she's now your slave

Or that you don't really appreciate her

You'd be personally digging your own grave

Killing sleep and sending peace afar

But then she should remain tolerantly humble

He is her lord even if he will still fumble.

I Believe

I believe in God, creator of mankind and the universe

I believe in Man, originator of doubts and inventions

I believe in Science: progenitor, server of today's needs.

I believe, O' yes, I truly and fully believe!

In the purpose of these all sensible three

Being as one, powerful as there can ever be.

I believe in His Image and Likeness I was made

But I'm blind, even to tomorrow's doubts and need

I believe; yet in the end, I am more likely to be dead.

I believe, so I expand this my terrestrial home

Building drones and the much respected dome

Thinking towers, computers, even the common broom.

I believe, Oh Yes! this is why I've been made to live

To work hard, enjoy this earth before I leave

Why blame me when it is you who won't believe?

Live My Life

I have lived a very full forty years

Yet to make the much needed difference;

I have worked hard and deep at the soil,

But in vain do I seem to search and toil.

A friendly sage once asked me with gloomy strain

"What do you seek? Tell me! What is your pain?"

I looked him in the eye with moistened sight

The sudden wetness revealing my plight.

"Weep not my friend, for your future is bright

Stress not your spirit, hold not your body tight;

Believe it is all well, never let your mind doubt

You'll live your life full and surely win the bout".

"Stop! Look up and dry your sad face of tears

Stand up! Confront your most deepest fears.

Push strong, remain steadfast and undaunted

Don't give up: know that the days are counted".

I rise up with renewed hope, joy and glee

Feeling a new strength surge within me;

I reflect on the wisdom of the man's words

And look up to behold the born again clouds.

Seeing a bright sky filled with promises,

I resolve a future without fear of many misses.

Determined to succeed, I conquer the clouts

Planning to work hard to trivialize my doubts.

For the presence of life today now assures me

That my success is granted and meant to be;

That the salt of my sweat will someday count

To bring about a much needed win to the bout.

When Will You Come To Me?

I want you, I need you

Yea, I'm ready for you

Yet you still make me wait

Anxiously, in deep sorry state.

O dear, when will you come to me?

I've waited long: pained and gloomy

I've been patient, but now I'm feisty:

For I have already knocked forty.

Do I at this age remain a fool

Do I break the horn of a live bull?

Do I kick the tall and very fat sky

Or the very depths of hell pry?

When then, will you come to me?

Is it that it may never really be?

Do I wait until I'm dry and grey,

Or possibly dead and in clay?

Tell me when and how to meet with you

Is it at the hour of the clouds of blue?

Or beyond the place of man's rearing?

Tell me now! For I'm almost done caring.

Mama Nigeria

I was born not with a silver spoon, but gold and diamonds

I live in the midst of plenty and abundance-

Splashing about in a free flow of milk and honey,

I glory in an amazing empire of oil, ore, hardcore and intrigues

Waiting and wasting all that nature has given to us.

My mother is an acclaimed giant from the region of the monkeys

Where buildings grow slowly and tomorrow's leaders die quickly

The woman of many parts and hundreds of children, my mother:

She is fit to shoot the skies but weak to raise the bow,

Her spears and arrows are sharpened but seldom used.

My mother whose children grab at the jugular

Fleecing all but her very life, the integral part of her existence;

Bleeding and crying, she pleads - "remain so is all I ask

For the sake of the fathers that founded you,

Who a hundred years ago, consorted for a single mother".

Yet they still bleed and milk her like there's no tomorrow.

Accepting as the norm to steal her jewelry to be fine.

The same children she keeps as one, squeeze with pillage;

Hating and fighting each other, they battle for superiority
Darting at themselves in diverse tongues and manners.

Some are even silly to ask "Where is the common destiny?"
Mama, tell them their destiny is in the oneness you preach
Tell them the ship long set sail, but uhuru is yet to be the song
Tell them to behave in their craving quest for your breast milk;
That a child who refuses his mother sleep will himself lie awake.

Remind them that you have borne us for a hundred years
That your own child will fight and die for a mother as big you
Tell them your strength and weakness is the who you are;
And that it'll take more than a hundred billion burbling children
To suck you dry, change your name, or reduce the size of you.

Oh Mama Nigeria! Wake up now, come forth and don't shy away
Rise up from your sleepy slumber for there is no more time
Please act, for the threats are much and the odds are high
Do not drip another drop of blood for these heady children
Tell us all to behave! Or Mama, it'll be wisdom to use your cane.

Have You Ever Dreamed

Have you ever dreamed

of a Nigeria where all is well;

Where the streets are cleaned,

and everywhere is safe to dwell?

Have you ever dreamed

of a Nigeria where promises are kept;

Where the leaders really want to lead,

achieving results both brave and apt?

Have you ever dreamed

of a Nigeria where peace and unity is secure;

Where tribal sentiment discords are doomed,

and terrorism and militancy become obscure?

Have you ever dreamed

of a Nigeria where children are cared for;

Where youths are skilled and well primed:

patriotic, not brooding over a dark yore?

Have you ever dreamed

of a Nigeria where aged care is available;

Where social security is set and assured,

and medicare is faithful and affordable?

Have you ever dreamed

of a Nigeria where industries thrive;

Where electric power is effectively spread,

and citizens access energy, and refineries survive?

Have you ever dreamed

of a Nigeria where corruption is abominable;

Where common resources are fully harnessed,

and the system's process is due and infallible?

I have dreamed and dreamt, till date, I still dream

of an invigorated nation, an even greater Nigeria;

A realm where the common masses reign supreme,

but each time, some others put it down as malaria.

The Yard

I grabbed my towel

Headed for the bathroom

I get close, but the queue is too long.

I change course and off to the loo I go

There too, I see a worm speed line

What do I do?

I shiver and clutch my bottom

Chei! Do I wait and soil myself?

Do I rush out and embrace the bush?

Do I run late for my scheduled meeting?

Or do I cheat and get there unclean

I curse myself and the wronging economy

I will be better off in a personal flat

And should have my private car too

I deserve comfort and security please,

And not to suffer throughout this life.

I have a right to make myself happy,

Therefore I must make this meet.

But then, how do I do it,

When I still need to poo?

What'd you do if you're in my shoe?

A Better Day

Good morning fine day

I know you slept well

For I can already see your shine

From the crack in my one room wall.

I hope you bring me better

For last night was a chiller,

Devoid of dreams and peace

As I tossed on my mat, praying it to end.

Now that you are here,

I don't want no rainy story

For I need your shining brilliance

To give warmth to my dying bones.

Though I wish you'll stay put till my end

I know you must come and go as ordained

And though I want to hug your warmth

You must soon push me away to the cold.

But even as go I must,

Do not starve my people of your time

And for all who'd abandoned me to die,

Please show them light, to see their wrong.

A Goodbye Story

You were my friend -
Long before you became my mother;
My confidant right until the end:
You taught me to cease to bother.

You were a good woman,
As humble as any can be;
Wise, disciplined, than many a man,
Generous, caring; so much, all did see.

You were indeed a blessing from the skies
A priceless gem, an invaluable personality;
Embodiment of kindness in paradise -
Role model; lover of peace and unity.

Words alone cannot describe you -
Nor can they wipe away our tears;
They cannot fill the vacuum left by you
Nor can they obliterate our fears.

Adeiu Auntie Oby,

Goodbye my mother-in-law,

I had known you barely for five years -

but I know you were the best I ever saw;

Good bye ma, enjoy eternal peace and grace.

You Still Live

I read the heart breaker first online

Ogbuehi dead! It was hard to believe -

The simple hand that propped many vine

Among Alaenyi people, no more to live.

I asked, and finally got to know the date

Thirtieth and thirty-first of July I heard -

Be there! I planned, but then I was late

Doubling my pain and bloating up my bad.

Sir Victor, you were more than a brother

Caring, encouraging, unlike most

To you, I was important, never a bother;

You will stand by me, not minding the cost.

I knew at some time you were sick,

But never saw it'd cause your transition;

I never knew your time was on fast track

Thus death became a far fetched notion.

Yes, you may be dead and gone

And they say Victor Oduocha is no more;

But in our minds, you will still live on

And your legacy will still rise to the fore.

Your patriotism: none will ever deny,

Nor that you hustled to make ends meet;

Your fraternal nature no one will ably belie,

Nor the loss for those in whom you made a beat.

Adieu, rest now brother and friend

The worries of earth are beyond you now;

May we fare well those you've left behind,

Until the day we meet after the final bow.

Adieu Grandma

My phone rang,

It was the news announced

The tears came,

Cascading down my cheeks

The pain stung,

Reality dawned on me

And so as we feared -

Mama Ukwu was no more.

Mama Mabel, the Diamond Mother,

You held us close to your bosom

When we grew up as kids;

You sang, you cooed, you played

You kept us happy, away from hurt.

You were never quick to scold,

Yet firm you remained in discipline;

You encouraged, prayed, never demeaning.

Mama Obazu, sweet grandmother,

Yours was a journey of love;

On compassion and strength,

And spiritual growth you stood.

True you're gone, but in our hearts you live still

My wife and I mourn you, the children miss you

The names you gave us we bear still-

Never to forget, knowing you are still with us

Adieu Mama! We love you to eternity.